Collins

easy le

Multiplication and division
bumper book

Ages 5–7

4 × 2 =

Brad Thompson

How to use this book

- Easy Learning bumper books help your child improve basic skills, build confidence and develop a love of learning.

- Find a quiet, comfortable place to work, away from distractions.

- Get into a routine of completing one or two bumper book pages with your child each day.

- At the end of each double page, ask your child to circle the star that matches how many questions they have completed:

Some = half or fewer   Most = more than half   All = all of the questions

- The progress certificate at the back of this book will help you and your child keep track of how many ★ have been circled.

- Encourage your child to work through all of the questions eventually and praise them for completing the progress certificate.

- The ability to recall and use times table facts is an essential skill and invaluable for many mathematical processes.

- Learning the times tables at an early age will give your child confidence with numbers.

Parent tip
Look out for tips on how to help your child learn.

- Ask your child to find and count the little mice that are hidden throughout this book.

- This will engage them with the pages of the book and get them interested in the activities.

(Don't count this one.)

Published by Collins
An imprint of HarperCollins*Publishers* Ltd
1 London Bridge Street
London SE1 9GF

Browse the complete Collins catalogue at www.collins.co.uk

© HarperCollins*Publishers* Ltd 2018

First published 2018

10 9 8 7 6 5 4 3

ISBN 9780008275471

British Library Cataloguing in Publication Data.

A Catalogue record for this publication is available from the British Library.

All images and illustrations are
© Shutterstock.com and
© HarperCollins*Publishers*

Author: Brad Thompson
Commissioning Editor: Michelle I'Anson
Project Manager: Rebecca Skinner
Cover Design: Sarah Duxbury
Text Design and Layout: QBS Learning
Production: Natalia Rebow
Printed by Martins the Printers

Contents

Counting in 2s on a number line

Counting in 2s on a number line will help you learn your 2 times table!

1 Start at 0 on the number line.
Count from left to right in 2s by making the frog jump.
Circle each number that the frog lands on.

0   1   2   3   4   5   6   7   8   9   10

2 Write the numbers that the frog landed on in the table below.
This is the start of your 2 times table!

Number of jumps	1	2	3	4	5
Number landed on	2				

3 Start at 12 on the number line.
Count from left to right in 2s by making the frog jump.
Circle each number that the frog lands on.

12   13   14   15   16   17   18   19   20   21   22   23   24

4 Write the numbers that the frog landed on in the table below.
This is the rest of your 2 times table!

Number of jumps	6	7	8	9	10	11	12
Number landed on	12						

5 Count forward in 2s and write the missing numbers.

0	2	4			10	12
8	10		14	16	18	
12	14	16	18	20		

Parent tip
Encourage your child to chant their two times table: 'One times two is two, ...'

6 Write all the numbers up to 24 on the path.
Use one colour for the numbers that you say when counting in 2s from 0.
Use a different colour for all the other numbers.

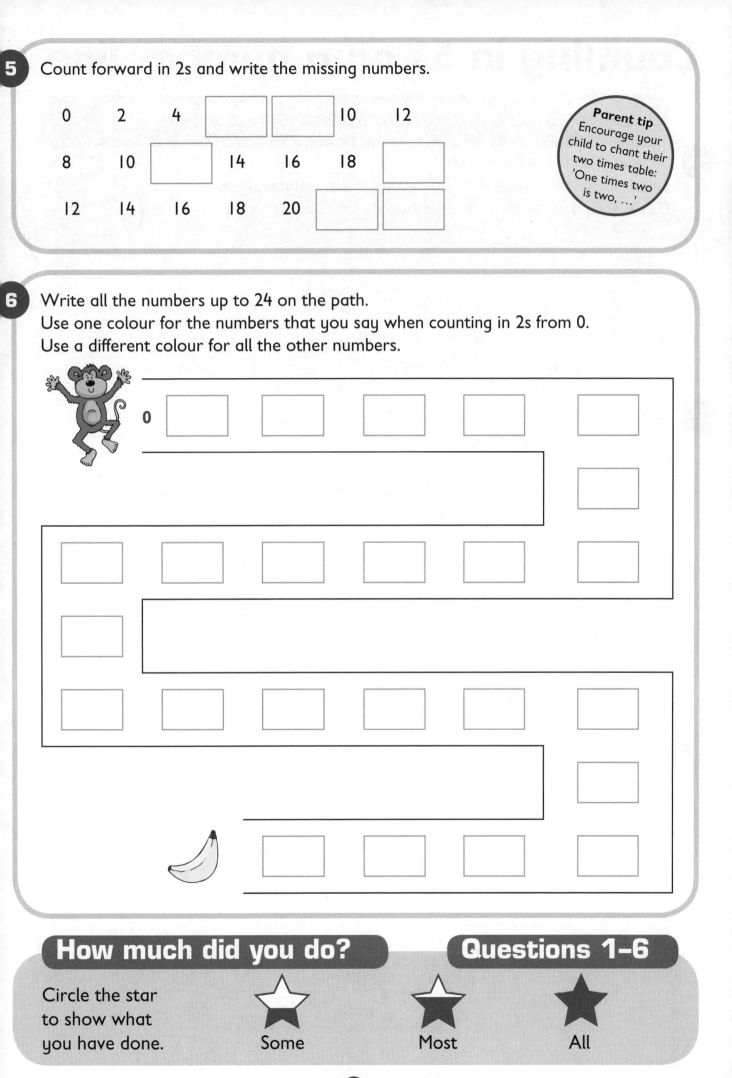

0

Counting in 5s on a number line

Counting in 5s on a number line will help you learn your 5 times table!

1 Start at 0 on the number line.
Count from left to right in 5s by making the grasshopper jump.
Circle each number that the grasshopper lands on.

0 1 2 3 4 5 6 7 8 9 10 11 12 13 14 15 16 17 18 19 20

2 Start at 5.
Add 5 each time and write the next number on the T-shirt.

5

3 Count forward in 5s and write the missing numbers.

0	5	10	15			30
10	15		25		35	
20			35	40	45	
30		40	45	50		

4 Start at 0.
Count forward in 5s.
Colour each square that you land on.

0	1	2	3	4	5	6	7	8	9	10	11	12	13	14	15	16	17	18

19

20

39	38	37	36	35	34	33	32	31	30	29	28	27	26	25	24	23	22	21

40

41

42	43	44	45	46	47	48	49	50	51	52	53	54	55	56	57	58	59	60

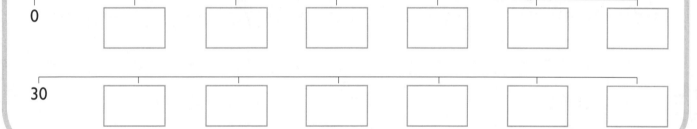

5 Start at 0.
Write the numbers from the coloured squares on the number lines.

0   [ ]   [ ]   [ ]   [ ]   [ ]   [ ]

30   [ ]   [ ]   [ ]   [ ]   [ ]   [ ]

6 Write the numbers from the number line in the table below.
This is your 5 times table!

Number of jumps	1	2	3	4	5	6	7	8	9	10	11	12
Number landed on	5											

How much did you do?   Questions 1–6

Circle the star to show what you have done.

 Some
 Most
 All

Counting in 10s on a number line

Counting in 10s on a number line will help you learn your 10 times table!

1 Start at 0. Draw a line to join the 10s in order.

Parent tip
Ask your child to count in tens on their fingers, with each finger representing 10.

2 Start at 10.
Add 10 each time and write the next number on the carriage.

3 Match each label to the correct number line.

| 8 jumps of 10 | 2 jumps of 10 | 4 jumps of 10 | 5 jumps of 10 |

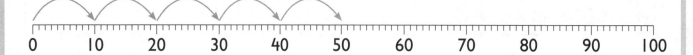

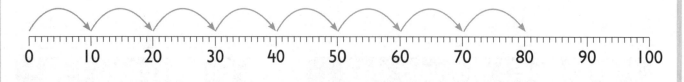

4 Write the missing numbers.

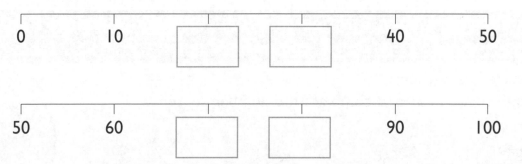

0   10   [ ]   [ ]   40   50

50   60   [ ]   [ ]   90   100

5 Here are two conveyor belts.
Add 10 each time.
Write the next number.

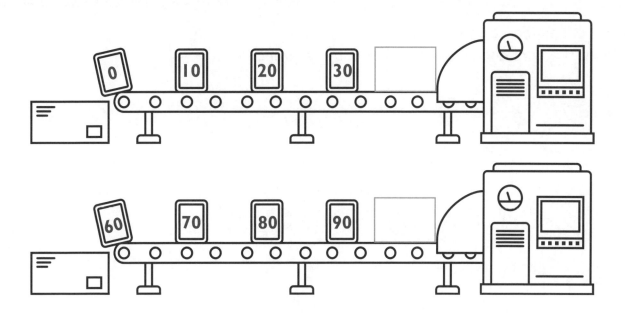

0   10   20   30   [ ]

60   70   80   90   [ ]

6 Count forward in 10s and write the missing numbers.

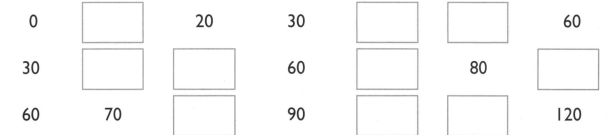

0   [ ]   20   30   [ ]   [ ]   60

30   [ ]   [ ]   60   [ ]   80   [ ]

60   70   [ ]   90   [ ]   [ ]   120

How much did you do?   ## Questions 1–6

Circle the star
to show what
you have done.

Some

Most

All

9

Counting objects in 2s

1 Each bicycle has 2 wheels.
Count the wheels in 2s and complete the number sentence.

Parent tip
Use objects that can be put into pairs, such as socks, shoes or gloves, to help your child count in twos.

4 × 2 =

2 Each animal has 2 ears.
Count the ears and complete the number sentence.

2 × 2 =

6 × 2 =

3 Each pot has 2 pencils in it.
Count the pencils in 2s and complete the number sentence.

1 × 2 =

10 × 2 =

4 Each dice is showing 2 spots.
Count the spots in 2s and complete the number sentence.

$9 \times 2 = $ ☐

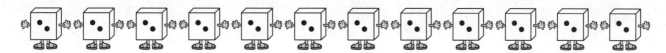

$12 \times 2 = $ ☐

---

5 Count in 2s to find the number of socks.
Complete the number sentence.

$8 \times 2 = $ ☐

---

6 Count in 2s to find the total value of the coins.

$3 \times 2p = $ ☐ p

$5 \times 2p = $ ☐ p

$7 \times 2p = $ ☐ p

How much did you do?   Questions 1–6

Circle the star
to show what
you have done.

 Some

 Most

 All

Counting objects in 5s

You can learn your 5 times table by repeatedly adding 5, e.g.
5 + 5 + 5 = 3 × 5 = 15!

1 Each glove has 5 fingers.
Count the fingers in 5s and complete the number sentence.

Parent tip
Ask your child to count how many fingers and toes your family has altogether, counting in fives.

6 × 5 = ▢

2 Each star has 5 points.
Count the points in 5s and complete the number sentence.

1 × 5 = ▢

10 × 5 = ▢

3 Each pentagon has 5 sides.
Count the number of sides in 5s and complete the number sentence.

7 × 5 = ▢

4 Each crown has 5 spikes.
Count the spikes in 5s and complete the number sentence.

☐ × ☐ = ☐

☐ × ☐ = ☐

5 Each dinosaur has 5 plates on its back.
Count the numbers of plates on the dinosaurs in 5s and complete the number sentence.

12 × 5 = ☐

6 Count in 5s to find the total value of the coins.

2 × 5p = ☐ p   4 × 5p = ☐ p

6 × 5p = ☐ p

Counting objects in 10s

You can learn your 10 times table by repeatedly adding 10, e.g.
10 + 10 + 10 = 3 × 10 = 30!

1 Each packet contains 10 erasers.
Count the erasers in 10s and complete the number sentence.

   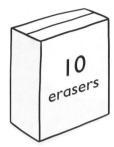

4 × 10 =

2 Each domino has 10 spots.
Count the spots in 10s and complete the number sentence.

 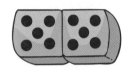

2 × 10 =

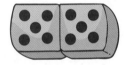    

5 × 10 =

3 Each crab has 10 legs.
Count the legs in 10s and complete the number sentence.

8 × 10 =

4 Each stack has 10 blocks.
Count the blocks in 10s and complete the number sentence.

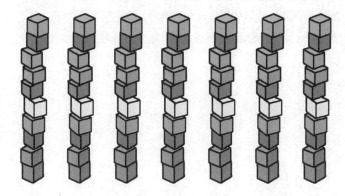 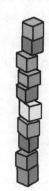

 × ☐ = ☐   ☐ × ☐ = ☐

5 Each flower has 10 petals.
Count the petals in 10s and complete the number sentence.

12 × 10 = ☐

6 Count in 10s to find the total value of the coins.

3 × 10p = ☐ p   5 × 10p = ☐ p

9 × 10p = ☐ p

How much did you do?   ## Questions 1–6

Circle the star to show what you have done.

 Some   Most    All

2s and 10s mixed practice

Try practising your 2 and 10 times tables together. Look out for the same products in both tables!

1 The first machine multiplies each number by 2.
The second machine multiplies each number by 10.
Write the numbers that come out of each machine.

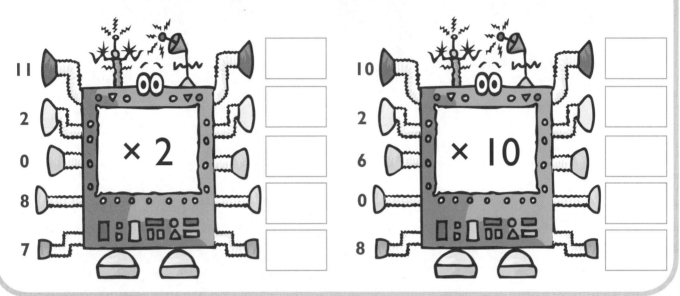

2 Each part of the bus has an answer on it.
Find the matching calculation on the code key to colour it in.

Code Key	
2 × 10	red
5 × 2	blue
8 × 2	grey
3 × 10	black
0 × 10	yellow

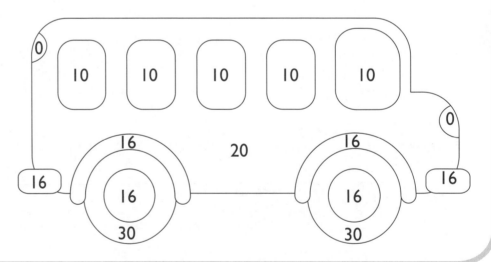

3 Tick the box if the number sentence is correct.
Put a cross if it is incorrect.

12 × 2 = 24 ☐   2 × 10 = 20 ☐   10 × 10 = 10 ☐

9 × 2 = 80 ☐   7 × 2 = 14 ☐   6 × 10 = 60 ☐

Progress check 1

Parent tip
If your child is feeling confident, time how long it takes them to complete the multiplications!

Can you answer all these calculations?

4 Write the answer to each calculation.
Use the number lines to help you if you need to.

0 2 4 6 8 10 12 14 16 18 20 22 24

0 5 10 15 20 25 30 35 40 45 50 55 60

0 10 20 30 40 50 60 70 80 90 100 110 120

0 × 2 =	8 × 10 =	2 × 2 =	0 × 5 =
4 × 2 =	9 × 10 =	4 × 5 =	7 × 2 =
9 × 5 =	12 × 10 =	10 × 2 =	8 × 5 =
12 × 2 =	3 × 2 =	12 × 5 =	0 × 10 =
3 × 10 =	6 × 2 =	5 × 2 =	6 × 5 =
7 × 5 =	5 × 10 =	8 × 2 =	6 × 10 =
10 × 10 =	1 × 5 =	2 × 5 =	1 × 10 =
2 × 10 =	3 × 5 =	4 × 10 =	11 × 2 =
10 × 5 =	7 × 10 =	1 × 2 =	5 × 5 =
11 × 5 =	11 × 10 =	9 × 2 =	

Score: __ / 39

How much did you do?   Question 1–4

Circle the star to show what you have done.

Some

Most

All

2 times table arrays

In an array, every row has the same number of objects in it and every column has the same number of objects in it.

1 Count the socks in the array.
Complete the number sentences.

$2 + 2 =$ ☐ $2 \times 2 =$ ☐

2 Count the daisies in this array.
Complete the number sentence.

$4 \times 2 =$ ☐

3 Colour the windows to show the array for 8×2.

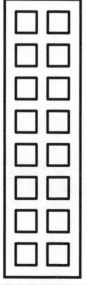

Parent tip
Call out a multiplication for the 2 times table and help your child to make an array using counters or other small objects.

$8 \times 2 =$ ☐

4 Count the shoes in this array.
Complete the number sentence.

$9 \times 2 =$ ☐

5 Some of the array is missing.
Draw some more counters so that it shows 11×2.
How many counters altogether?

$11 \times 2 =$ ☐

6 Now draw an array to show 12×2.
Write the matching number sentence.
You can draw any objects you like to make your array!

☐ × ☐ = ☐

5 times table arrays

Arrays can be a useful way to represent times tables.

1 Count the tennis balls in this array.
Complete the number sentence.

1 × 5 = ☐

2 Count the cricket balls in this array.
Complete the number sentence.

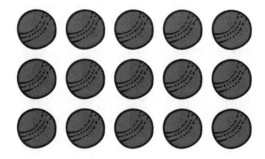

☐ × 5 = ☐

3 Colour 5 columns of squares to show 7 × 5 as an array.

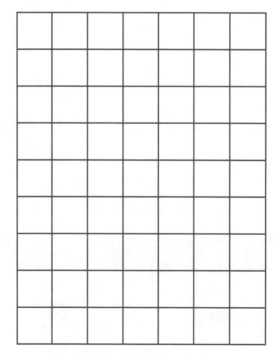

Parent tip
Encourage your child to make arrays using household objects.

4 Look at this array. Tick the box next to the matching calculation.

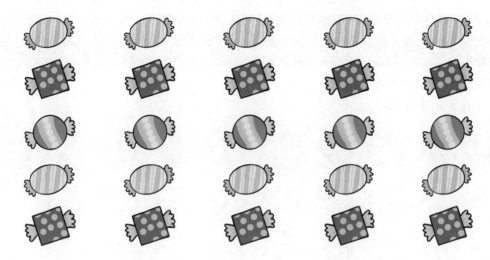

4 × 5 ☐   1 × 5 ☐   5 × 5 ☐   7 × 5 ☐   11 × 5 ☐

5 Draw a line to match each calculation to the correct array.

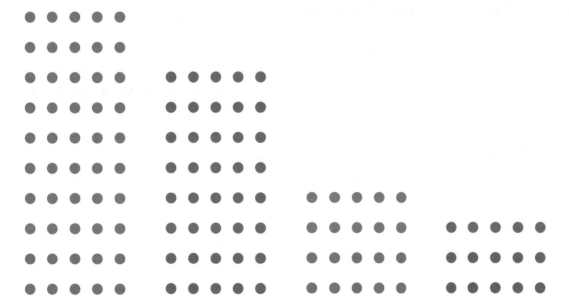

3 × 5   4 × 5   8 × 5   10 × 5

How much did you do?   **Questions 1–5**

Circle the star
to show what
you have done.   Some   Most    All

21

10 times table arrays

You can use an array to show what happens when you keep adding the same number.

1 Count the footballs in this array.
Complete the number sentence.

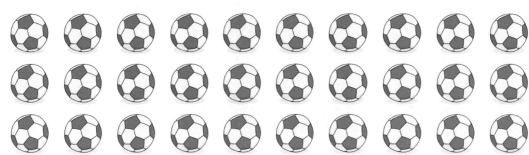

$3 \times 10 = \boxed{}$

2 Add more dots to the array to show 4×10.
Complete the number sentence.

$4 \times 10 = \boxed{}$

3 Look at each picture.
Complete the number sentence for each one.

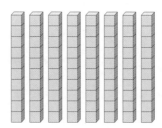

$1 \times 10 = \boxed{10}$

$\boxed{} \times \boxed{} = \boxed{}$

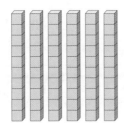

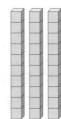

$\boxed{} \times \boxed{} = \boxed{}$

$\boxed{} \times \boxed{} = \boxed{}$

4 Write two number sentences for each array.

$$\boxed{} \times \boxed{} = \boxed{}$$

$$\boxed{} \times \boxed{} = \boxed{}$$

$$\boxed{} \times \boxed{} = \boxed{}$$

$$\boxed{} \times \boxed{} = \boxed{}$$

5 Draw a line to match each calculation to the correct array.

1 × 10   4 × 10   7 × 10

6 In the grid, draw the array for 7 × 10.
You can draw anything you like in each square!

Doubling numbers

When doubling, you are finding **2** lots of something. So, any number multiplied by **2** is doubled.

1 Count the pairs of objects.
Multiply the number of pairs by 2.

6 × 2 =   8 × 2 =   3 × 2 =

Parent tip
Count out a number of objects. Ask your child to double the number by counting out the same amount again.

2 The two dice in each pair show the same number.
Multiply the number by 2 to show the total score.

   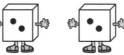

3 × 2 =   2 × 2 =   6 × 2 =

   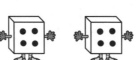

1 × 2 =   4 × 2 =   5 × 2 =

3 Count the dots on the butterfly's wing.
Draw the same number of dots on the other wing.
Write the missing numbers.

Double ☐ = ☐   Double ☐ = ☐   Double ☐ = ☐

4 The top bar shows the total.
The two bars under it contain matching numbers that make the same total.
Write the missing numbers.

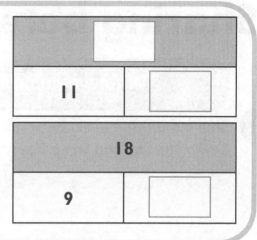

5 The spots in the arrays are in two colours.
Complete the number sentence to show the double.

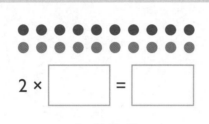

$2 \times \boxed{} = \boxed{}$

$2 \times \boxed{} = \boxed{}$

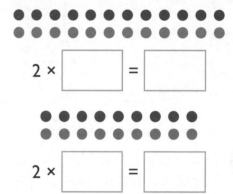

$2 \times \boxed{} = \boxed{}$

$2 \times \boxed{} = \boxed{}$

6 See how quickly you can make your way around the race track by completing the calculations.

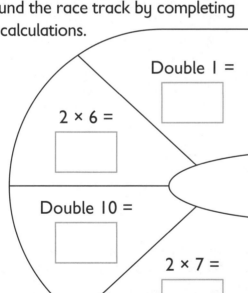
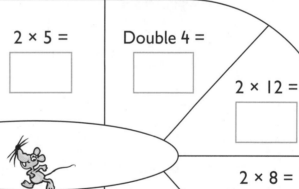
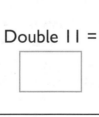
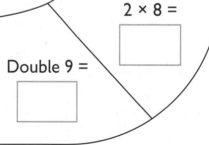

Double 1 =

2 × 5 =

Double 4 =

2 × 6 =

2 × 12 =

Double 10 =

2 × 8 =

2 × 7 =

Double 11 =

Double 9 =

Sharing between 2

1 Share the fish equally between the 2 bowls.
Draw the fish and write how many there are in each bowl.

[ ] fish   [ ] fish

Parent tip
Ask your child to share an even number of objects between two bowls.

2 Share the biscuits equally between the 2 jars.
Draw the biscuits and complete the number sentence.

16 shared by 2 = [ ]

3 Share the counters equally between 2 groups.
Draw the counters and write the missing number.

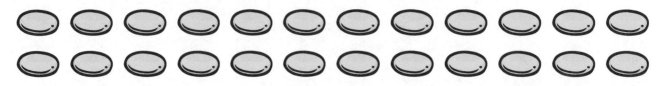

24 shared by 2 = [ ]

4 The top bar shows the whole.
Share the whole equally between the two lower bars.

10	
5	5

20

30

5 Write the missing numbers to balance the scales.

14 shared by 2

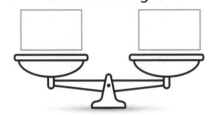

32 shared by 2

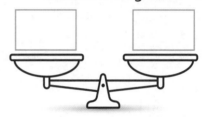

24 shared by 2

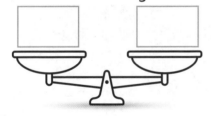

40 shared by 2

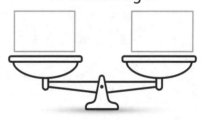

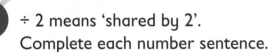

6 ÷ 2 means 'shared by 2'.
Complete each number sentence.

$36 ÷ 2 = \boxed{}$ $58 ÷ 2 = \boxed{}$ $60 ÷ 2 = \boxed{}$

$\boxed{} = 20 ÷ 2$ $\boxed{} = 44 ÷ 2$ $\boxed{} = 70 ÷ 2$

How much did you do?   Questions 1–6

Circle the star
to show what
you have done.

Some

Most

All

Sharing between 5

1 Share the 15 letters equally between the 5 houses.
Draw the letters and write how many each house gets.

Parent tip
Count out a multiple of five objects and ask your child to share them between five.

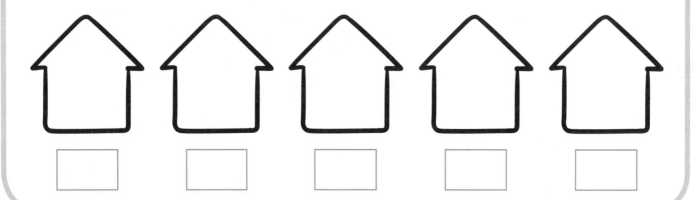

2 Share the treasure equally between the pirates.
Draw the coins and write how many coins each pirate gets.

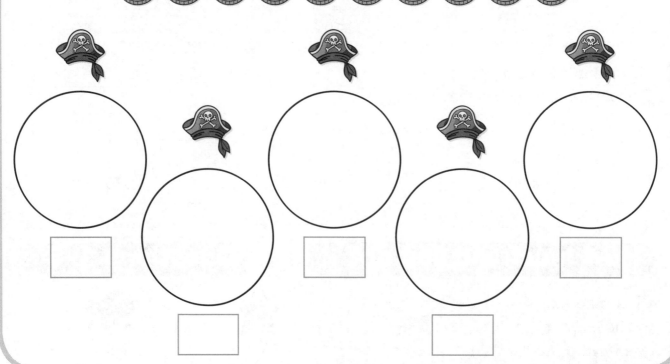

3 Draw a line to match each calculation to the correct answer.

(45 shared by 5)   (10 shared by 5)   (20 shared by 5)

(2)   (4)   (9)

4 The top bar shows the whole.
Share the whole equally between the 5 parts below.

40				

25				

30				

5 Write the missing numbers.

$35 \div 5 =$ ☐ $50 \div 5 =$ ☐ $45 \div 5 =$ ☐

☐ $= 30 \div 5$ ☐ $= 40 \div 5$ ☐ $= 55 \div 5$

How much did you do?   **Questions 1–5**

Circle the star
to show what
you have done.

 Some   ⭐ Most   ⭐ All

Sharing between 10

1 Share the strawberries equally between the 10 boxes.
Draw the strawberries and write how many are in each box.

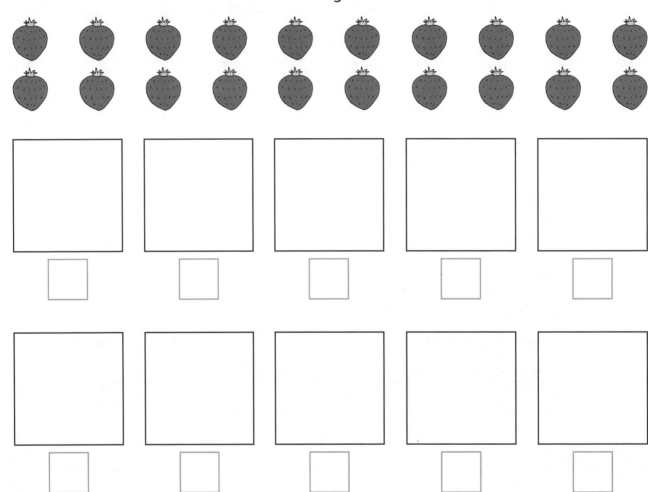

2 Share the footballs equally between the 10 children.
Draw the footballs and write how many each child gets.

3 The top bar shows the whole.
Share the whole equally between the 10 parts below.

Parent tip
Ask your child to share different objects (multiples of ten) equally between 10.

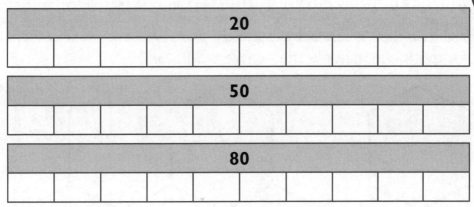

4 Choose the correct answer and draw a smiley face in the circle.

10 shared by 10 =   8 ◯   1 ◯   3 ◯

60 shared by 10 =   6 ◯   7 ◯   1 ◯

30 shared by 10 =   9 ◯   5 ◯   3 ◯

5 All the numbers that go into the machine are shared by 10.
Write the numbers that come out of the machine in the boxes.

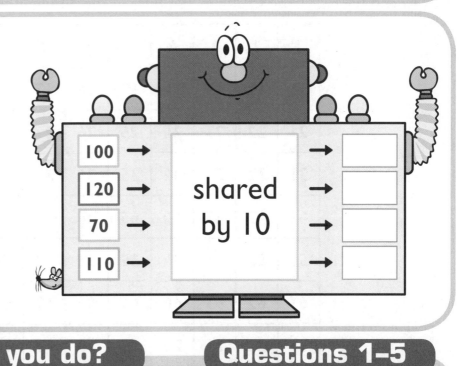

How much did you do?   Questions 1–5

Circle the star to show what you have done.

 Some   Most   All

5s and 10s mixed practice

Practise multiplying by 5 and 10. What do you notice about the numbers?

1 Follow the footpath and multiply the numbers by 5 or 10.

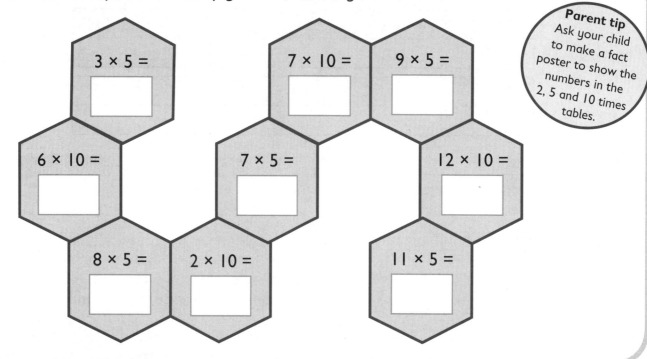

3 × 5 =

7 × 10 =

9 × 5 =

6 × 10 =

7 × 5 =

12 × 10 =

8 × 5 =

2 × 10 =

11 × 5 =

Parent tip
Ask your child to make a fact poster to show the numbers in the 2, 5 and 10 times tables.

2 Draw a circle around all the numbers in the 5 times table.
Draw a triangle around all the numbers in the 10 times table.

1	2	3	4	5	6	7	8	9	10
11	12	13	14	15	16	17	18	19	20
21	22	23	24	25	26	27	28	29	30
31	32	33	34	35	36	37	38	39	40
41	42	43	44	45	46	47	48	49	50
51	52	53	54	55	56	57	58	59	60
61	62	63	64	65	66	67	68	69	70
71	72	73	74	75	76	77	78	79	80
81	82	83	84	85	86	87	88	89	90
91	92	93	94	95	96	97	98	99	100

Progress check 2

3 Write the answer to each calculation.

Parent tip
If your child is feeling confident, time how long it takes them to complete the divisions!

2 ÷ 2 = ☐   80 ÷ 10 = ☐   2 ÷ 1 = ☐   4 ÷ 2 = ☐

8 ÷ 2 = ☐   90 ÷ 10 = ☐   20 ÷ 5 = ☐   14 ÷ 2 = ☐

45 ÷ 5 = ☐   120 ÷ 10 = ☐   20 ÷ 2 = ☐   40 ÷ 5 = ☐

24 ÷ 2 = ☐   6 ÷ 2 = ☐   60 ÷ 5 = ☐   10 ÷ 2 = ☐

30 ÷ 10 = ☐   12 ÷ 2 = ☐   10 ÷ 5 = ☐   30 ÷ 5 = ☐

35 ÷ 5 = ☐   50 ÷ 10 = ☐   16 ÷ 2 = ☐   60 ÷ 10 = ☐

100 ÷ 10 = ☐   5 ÷ 5 = ☐   10 ÷ 1 = ☐   10 ÷ 10 = ☐

20 ÷ 10 = ☐   15 ÷ 5 = ☐   40 ÷ 10 = ☐   22 ÷ 2 = ☐

50 ÷ 5 = ☐   70 ÷ 10 = ☐   5 ÷ 1 = ☐   25 ÷ 5 = ☐

55 ÷ 5 = ☐   110 ÷ 10 = ☐   18 ÷ 2 = ☐

Score: __ / 39

How much did you do?   ## Question 1- 3

Circle the star
to show what
you have done.

Some

Most

All

Halving numbers

When halving numbers, you are sharing or dividing by 2.

1 Draw rings to divide all the objects into 2 equal groups.
Complete the number sentence.

$4 \div 2 =$

$6 \div 2 =$

$10 \div 2 =$

Parent tip
Give your child an even number of objects and ask them to halve the set.

2 Draw rings to divide each array into 2 equal groups.
Complete the number sentence.

• • • • • • • •
• • • • • • • •

$16 \div 2 =$

• • • • • • • • • • • •
• • • • • • • • • • • •

$24 \div 2 =$

• •
• •

$4 \div 2 =$

3 Halve these numbers.

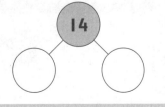 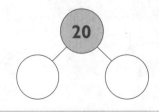 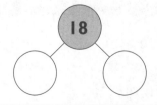

4 Halve each of the numbers and then complete the division number sentence.

Half of 22 = [ ]   Half of 40 = [ ]   Half of 90 = [ ]

22 ÷ [ ] = [ ]   40 ÷ [ ] = [ ]   90 ÷ [ ] = [ ]

5 Write the missing numbers.

Half of 12 = [ ]   10 ÷ 2 = [ ]   Half of 100 = [ ]

14 ÷ 2 = [ ]   Half of 20 = [ ]   Half of 18 = [ ]

Half of 4 = [ ]   40 ÷ 2 = [ ]   Half of 70 = [ ]

60 ÷ 2 = [ ]   Half of 50 = [ ]   Half of 22 = [ ]

6 Write the missing numbers.

Half of 24 = 12   So, 24 ÷ 2 = [ ] and 24 ÷ [ ] = 2

Half of 20 = 10   So, 20 ÷ 2 = [ ] and 20 ÷ [ ] = 2

Half of 40 = 20   So, 40 ÷ 2 = [ ] and 40 ÷ [ ] = 2

Half of 14 = 7   So, 14 ÷ 2 = [ ] and 14 ÷ [ ] = 2

Half of 30 = 15   So, 30 ÷ 2 = [ ] and 30 ÷ [ ] = 2

Half of 80 = 40   So, 80 ÷ 2 = [ ] and 80 ÷ [ ] = 2

How much did you do?   Questions 1–6

Circle the star to show what you have done.

 Some   Most   All

Counting backward on a number line

You can divide by repeatedly subtracting the same amount. This can be shown on a number line.

1 Start at 10. Count backward in 2s by making the frog jump.
Count how many jumps you need to reach 0 and complete the number sentence.

```
0    1    2    3    4    5    6    7    8    9    10
```

$10 \div 2 = $ ☐

Parent tip
Encourage your child to count backward from different tens numbers in 2s, 5s and 10s.

2 Start at 60.
Count backward in 5s and draw each jump.
Count how many jumps you need to reach 0.

```
0   5   10   15   20   25   30   35   40   45   50   55   60
```

$60 \div 5 = $ ☐

3 Start at 50.
Make the dolphin jump over each object in 10s.
How many jumps does it take to reach 0?

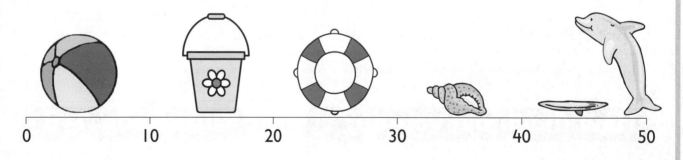

```
0        10        20        30        40        50
```

$50 \div 10 = $ ☐

4 Start at the biggest number shown in the calculation and jump back in 2s to 0.
Count the number of jumps and complete the number sentence.

| 0 | 2 | 4 | 6 | 8 | 10 | 12 | 14 | 16 | 18 | 20 | 22 | 24 |

$24 \div 2 =$ ☐

| 0 | 2 | 4 | 6 | 8 | 10 | 12 | 14 | 16 | 18 | 20 | 22 | 24 |

$16 \div 2 =$ ☐

5 Start at the biggest number shown in the calculation and jump back in 5s to 0.
Count the number of jumps and complete the number sentence.

| 0 | 5 | 10 | 15 | 20 | 25 | 30 | 35 | 40 | 45 | 50 | 55 | 60 |

$35 \div 5 =$ ☐

| 0 | 5 | 10 | 15 | 20 | 25 | 30 | 35 | 40 | 45 | 50 | 55 | 60 |

$55 \div 5 =$ ☐

6 Start at the biggest number shown in the calculation and jump back in 10s to 0.
Count the number of jumps and complete the number sentence.

| 0 | 10 | 20 | 30 | 40 | 50 | 60 | 70 | 80 | 90 |

$90 \div 10 =$ ☐

| 0 | 10 | 20 | 30 | 40 | 50 | 60 | 70 | 80 | 90 |

$40 \div 10 =$ ☐

Grouping in 2s

1 Draw rings to group all the socks into 2s.
Complete the number sentence.

[ ] groups of 2

Parent tip
Ask your child to divide an even number of objects into groups of two and then count the number of groups.

2 Draw rings to group all the gloves into 2s.
Complete the number sentence.

[ ] groups of 2

3 Draw rings to group all the shoes into 2s.
Complete the number sentence.

[ ] groups of 2

4 Draw a line to match each calculation to the correct answer.

14 grouped into 2s		(11)
18 grouped into 2s		(10)
20 grouped into 2s		(7)
22 grouped into 2s		(12)
24 grouped into 2s		(9)

5 All the items have been grouped into 2s.
Complete the number sentence for each picture.

☐ = ☐ groups of 2   ☐ = ☐ groups of 2

☐ = ☐ groups of 2   ☐ = ☐ groups of 2

6 Write the missing numbers.

12 can be grouped into ☐ groups of 2.

4 can be grouped into ☐ groups of 2.

16 can be grouped into ☐ groups of 2.

2 can be grouped into ☐ group of 2.

Grouping in 5s

When dividing by 5, you can make groups of 5 and see how many groups you have.

1 Draw rings to group all the cricket balls into 5s.
Complete the number sentence.

[ ] groups of 5

2 Draw rings to group all the footballs into 5s.
Complete the number sentence.

[ ] groups of 5

3 Draw rings to group all the toy cars into 5s.
Write the missing numbers.

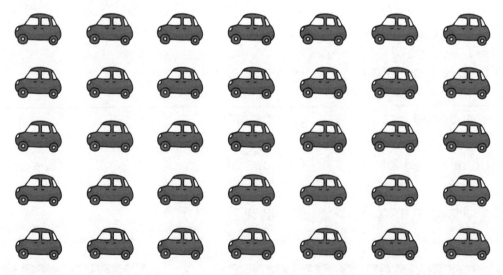

There are [ ] groups of 5 in 35.

35 ÷ 5 = [ ]

4 The objects have been grouped into 5s.
Complete the number sentence for each picture.

 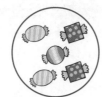

10 ÷ 5 = ☐   20 ÷ 5 = ☐

5 Here is part of a 100 square.
Group all the numbers into 5s.
The first group has been done
for you.

1	2	3	4	5	6	7	8	9	10
11	12	13	14	15	16	17	18	19	20
21	22	23	24	25	26	27	28	29	30
31	32	33	34	35	36	37	38	39	40
41	42	43	44	45	46	47	48	49	50
51	52	53	54	55	56	57	58	59	60

There are ☐ groups of 5 in 60.

6 All the numbers that
go into the machine
are grouped into 5s.
Write how many groups
are made from each
number.

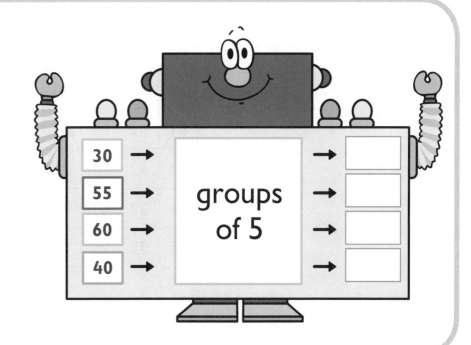

30 → groups of 5 → ☐
55 → → ☐
60 → → ☐
40 → → ☐

Grouping in 10s

When dividing by 10, you can make groups of 10 and see how many groups you have.

1 Draw rings to group all the crayons into 10s.
Complete the number sentence.

Parent tip
Give your child sets of 20, 30 and 40 small objects (dried pasta works well). Ask them how many groups of 10 they can make from each set.

[ ] groups of 10

2 Here is a 100 square. Group the numbers into 10s. The first group has been done for you.

1	2	3	4	5	6	7	8	9	10
11	12	13	14	15	16	17	18	19	20
21	22	23	24	25	26	27	28	29	30
31	32	33	34	35	36	37	38	39	40
41	42	43	44	45	46	47	48	49	50
51	52	53	54	55	56	57	58	59	60
61	62	63	64	65	66	67	68	69	70
71	72	73	74	75	76	77	78	79	80
81	82	83	84	85	86	87	88	89	90
91	92	93	94	95	96	97	98	99	100

There are [ ] groups of 10 in 100.

3 Here is an array for the number 40.
How many groups of 10 are there?

40 = [ ] groups of 10

4   Group the counters in this array into 10s.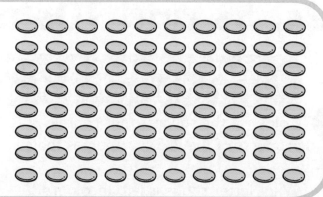
Write the missing numbers.

There are [ ] groups of 10 in 80.

80 ÷ 10 = [ ]

---

5   Match each array to the correct number sentence.
Complete the number sentence.

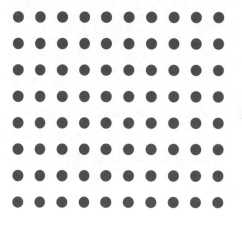

100 ÷ 10 = [ ]   60 ÷ 10 = [ ]   30 ÷ 10 = [ ]

---

6   Write the missing numbers.

There are [ ] groups of 10 in 90.   There are [ ] groups of 10 in 50.

90 ÷ 10 = [ ]   50 ÷ 10 = [ ]

There are [ ] groups of 10 in 70.   There are [ ] groups of 10 in 40.

70 ÷ 10 = [ ]   40 ÷ 10 = [ ]

How much did you do?   Questions 1–6

Circle the star
to show what
you have done.

          ★

Some   Most   All

2s, 5s and 10s mixed practice

Try practising your 2, 5 and 10 times tables together. Look out for products that appear in all three tables!

1 Colour in the squares that contain products of the 2, 5 or 10 times tables.

What letter shape is left uncoloured?

_____

11	20	56	12	87
70	3	30	61	40
6	25	37	10	15
35	99	5	49	80
1	14	18	24	29

Parent tip
Ask your child to write a song or poem about the 2, 5 and 10 times tables.

2 The dog wants to eat some dog treats.
He can only eat a treat if it has a product of the 2, 5 or 10 times tables on it.
Colour in the treats that the dog can eat!

 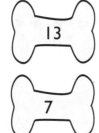 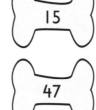 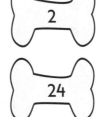  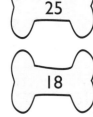

13   15   2   10   25

7   47   24   11   18

3 Write the following numbers in the correct box to show if they are in the 2, 5 or 10 times table. Some numbers will go in more than one box.

12   2   50   8   70   35   14   100   25   22   60   45

× 2	× 5	× 10

Progress check 3

4 Write the answer to each calculation.

0 × 2 = ☐   8 × 10 = ☐   2 × 2 = ☐   0 × 5 = ☐

4 × 2 = ☐   9 × 10 = ☐   4 × 5 = ☐   7 × 2 = ☐

9 × 5 = ☐   12 × 10 = ☐   10 × 2 = ☐   8 × 5 = ☐

12 × 2 = ☐   3 × 2 = ☐   12 × 5 = ☐   0 × 10 = ☐

3 × 10 = ☐   6 × 2 = ☐   5 × 2 = ☐   6 × 5 = ☐

7 × 5 = ☐   5 × 10 = ☐   8 × 2 = ☐   6 × 10 = ☐

10 × 10 = ☐   1 × 5 = ☐   2 × 5 = ☐   1 × 10 = ☐

2 × 10 = ☐   3 × 5 = ☐   4 × 10 = ☐   11 × 2 = ☐

10 × 5 = ☐   7 × 10 = ☐   1 × 2 = ☐   5 × 5 = ☐

11 × 5 = ☐   11 × 10 = ☐   9 × 2 = ☐

Parent tip
If you timed Progress check 1, time this one to see if your child can complete the multiplications more quickly.

Score: __ / 39

How much did you do?   ## Question 1–4

Circle the star to show what you have done.

 Some

 Most

 All

Problem solving and reasoning 1

Use facts for the 2 times table to solve these problems!

1 Write the total amount of money in each purse.

☐ p

☐ p

2 Ibrahim has 14 toy cars.
He shares them between 2 friends.

How many cars does each friend get?

☐ cars

3 12 gloves are left on a table.
They are in matching pairs.
Each pair belongs to a different child.

How many children left their gloves on the table?

☐ children

4 Jenny needs 24 football cards to complete her collection.
Cards are sold in packs of 2.

How many packs does she need to buy?

☐ packs

5 There are 12 bicycles in a rack.

How many wheels are there altogether?

☐ wheels

6 There are 18 wellies in Class 3's cloakroom.
The wellies are in matching pairs.
Each pair belongs to a different child.

How many children from Class 3 brought wellies to school today?

☐ children

Problem solving and reasoning 2

Use facts for the 5 times table to solve these problems!

1 Find the total amount of money in each purse.

[ ] p

[ ] p

2 Jenny rolls a dice 3 times.
Each time she scores 5.

What is Jenny's total score?

[ ]

3 It is Sports Day at school.
50 children are split into teams of 5.

How many teams are there altogether?

[ ] teams

4 A birthday party costs £5 per child.
Fatima wants 9 of her friends to come to her party.

How much will the party cost altogether, including Fatima?

£ [ ]

5 A tub contains 60 marbles.
The marbles are shared equally between 5 children.

How many marbles does each child get?

[ ] marbles

6 There are 7 tables in a classroom.
Each table needs 5 whiteboard pens.

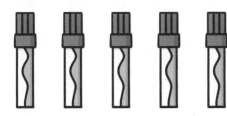

How many whiteboard pens are needed altogether?

[ ] pens

How much did you do?   **Questions 1–6**

Circle the star
to show what
you have done.

 Some   Most   All

Problem solving and reasoning 3

Use facts for the 10 times table to solve these problems!

1 Find the total amount of money in each purse.

$\boxed{}$ p

Parent tip
Ask your child to talk you through how they are going to solve the problem.

$\boxed{}$ p

2 There are 4 judges at a dance competition.
Each judge gives a dancer 10 points.

How many points does the dancer score altogether?

$\boxed{}$ points

3 There are 10 sweets in a packet.
A box contains 10 packets of sweets.

How many sweets are in the box altogether?

$\boxed{}$ sweets

4 A school orders 80 glue sticks.
Each class will get 10 glue sticks.

How many classes will get glue sticks?

☐ classes

5 A group of friends go ten-pin bowling.
There are 12 bowling alleys and 10 pins in each alley.

How many pins are there altogether?

☐ pins

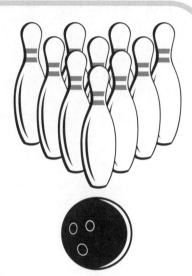

6 An art box contains 10 crayons.
A shop orders 6 art boxes.

How many crayons will be delivered?

☐ crayons

How much did you do?   Questions 1–6

Circle the star
to show what
you have done.

 Some    Most   All

51

Multiply and divide by 10

When making a number 10 times bigger or smaller, the digits appear to move to the left (×10) or right (÷10).

1 Multiply the numbers by 10.

Tens	Ones
	3
	2
	5
	7
	9

× 10

Tens	Ones
3	0

Parent tip
Get your child to count in tens if they find this hard.

2 Divide the numbers by 10.

Tens	Ones
2	0
3	0
4	0
6	0
8	0

÷ 10

Tens	Ones
	2

3 Write the missing numbers.

$6 \times 10 = $ ⬚   So, ⬚ $\div 10 = $ ⬚

$1 \times 10 = $ ⬚   So, ⬚ $\div 10 = $ ⬚

$12 \times 10 = $ ⬚   So, ⬚ $\div 10 = $ ⬚

$5 \times 10 = $ ⬚   So, ⬚ $\div 10 = $ ⬚

4 Write ×10 or ÷10 in each box.

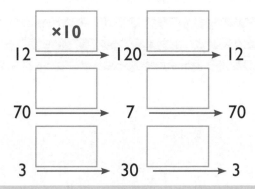
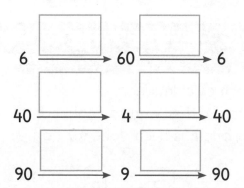

5 Write the answers.

6 ──ten times bigger──→ **60**

10 ──ten times smaller──→ ☐

9 ──ten times bigger──→ ☐

80 ──ten times smaller──→ ☐

120 ──ten times smaller──→ ☐

5 ──ten times bigger──→ ☐

60 ──ten times smaller──→ ☐

3 ──ten times bigger──→ ☐

6 Follow the footpath by multiplying or dividing the numbers by 10. You could even race a friend!

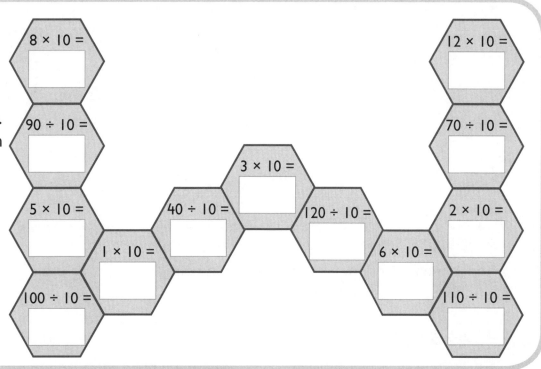

Commutativity

Some calculations can be carried out in any order and in many ways. However, others cannot.

1 Solve each calculation.
Then find another way to complete it.
The first one has been done for you.

$5 \times 2 = \boxed{10}$ $\boxed{2} \times 5 = \boxed{10}$

$9 \times 5 = \boxed{}$ $\boxed{} \times 9 = \boxed{}$

$10 \times 2 = \boxed{}$ $\boxed{} \times 10 = \boxed{}$

$3 \times 10 = \boxed{}$ $\boxed{} \times 3 = \boxed{}$

2 Write a division that is the reverse of each multiplication.
The first one has been done for you.

$7 \times 2 = 14$ $14 \div \boxed{2} = 7$

$6 \times 5 = 30$ $30 \div \boxed{} = 6$

$5 \times 10 = 50$ $50 \div \boxed{} = 5$

Parent tip
Write the numbers from a calculation on three separate cards. Encourage your child to move them into different positions to make new number sentences!

3 For each multiplication, write two division calculations using the same numbers.
The first one has been done for you.

$4 \times 5 = 20$ $20 \div 5 = \boxed{4}$ $20 \div 4 = \boxed{5}$

$7 \times 2 = 14$ $14 \div 2 = \boxed{}$ $14 \div 7 = \boxed{}$

$9 \times 10 = 90$ $90 \div 10 = \boxed{}$ $90 \div 9 = \boxed{}$

4 For each multiplication, write two division calculations using the same numbers. The first one has been done for you.

$12 \times 2 = 24$ | 24 | $\div\, 2 =$ | 12 | | 24 | $\div\, 12 =$ | 2 |

$8 \times 5 = 40$ | | $\div\, 5 =$ | | | | $\div\, 8 =$ | |

$9 \times 10 = 90$ | | $\div\, 10 =$ | | | | $\div\, 9 =$ | |

5 Complete each calculation.
Then use the same numbers to write another multiplication and two divisions.

$8 \quad \times \quad 2 \quad = \Box$

$\Box \quad \times \quad \Box \quad = \Box$

$\Box \quad \div \quad \Box \quad = \Box$

$\Box \quad \div \quad \Box \quad = \Box$

$11 \quad \times \quad 5 \quad = \Box$

$\Box \quad \times \quad \Box \quad = \Box$

$\Box \quad \div \quad \Box \quad = \Box$

$\Box \quad \div \quad \Box \quad = \Box$

6 Use each set of three numbers to write two multiplication and two division calculations.

7   10   70

$\Box \quad \times \quad \Box \quad = \Box$

$\Box \quad \times \quad \Box \quad = \Box$

$\Box \quad \div \quad \Box \quad = \Box$

$\Box \quad \div \quad \Box \quad = \Box$

5   12   60

$\Box \quad \times \quad \Box \quad = \Box$

$\Box \quad \times \quad \Box \quad = \Box$

$\Box \quad \div \quad \Box \quad = \Box$

$\Box \quad \div \quad \Box \quad = \Box$

How much did you do?   Questions 1–6

Circle the star to show what you have done.

 Some

 Most

 All

Exploring arrays and commutativity

Arrays are really important: you can use them to count in 1s, count in groups and multiply and divide numbers.

1 Match each calculation to the correct array.

2 + 2 + 2 + 2   5 + 5 + 5   10 + 10

2 Match each multiplication to the correct array.

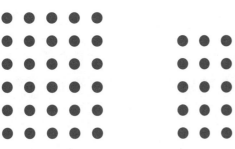

Parent tip
Encourage your child to explore repeated addition by placing objects on squared paper to make rows and columns.

5 × 10   8 × 2   6 × 5

3 Write how many groups there are in each array.

[ ] groups of 2   [ ] groups of 2   [ ] groups of 2

4 Write how many groups there are.
This time there are two number sentences to complete for each array.

[ ] groups of [ ]   [ ] groups of [ ]   [ ] groups of [ ]

[ ] groups of [ ]   [ ] groups of [ ]   [ ] groups of [ ]

5 Find one more multiplication sentence and one more division sentence for the array.

$10 \times 5 = 50$

[ ] × [ ] = [ ]

$50 \div 5 = 10$

[ ] ÷ [ ] = [ ]

6 Write two multiplication and two division sentences for the array.

[ ] × [ ] = [ ]

[ ] × [ ] = [ ]

[ ] ÷ [ ] = [ ]

[ ] ÷ [ ] = [ ]

How much did you do?   Questions 1–6

Circle the star to show what you have done.

 Some

Most

 All

Progress check 4

1 Write the answer to each calculation.

2 ÷ 2 = ☐   80 ÷ 10 = ☐   2 ÷ 1 = ☐   4 ÷ 2 = ☐

8 ÷ 2 = ☐   90 ÷ 10 = ☐   20 ÷ 5 = ☐   14 ÷ 2 = ☐

45 ÷ 5 = ☐   120 ÷ 10 = ☐   20 ÷ 2 = ☐   40 ÷ 5 = ☐

24 ÷ 2 = ☐   6 ÷ 2 = ☐   60 ÷ 5 = ☐   10 ÷ 2 = ☐

30 ÷ 10 = ☐   12 ÷ 2 = ☐   10 ÷ 5 = ☐   30 ÷ 5 = ☐

35 ÷ 5 = ☐   50 ÷ 10 = ☐   16 ÷ 2 = ☐   60 ÷ 10 = ☐

100 ÷ 10 = ☐   5 ÷ 5 = ☐   10 ÷ 1 = ☐   10 ÷ 10 = ☐

20 ÷ 10 = ☐   15 ÷ 5 = ☐   40 ÷ 10 = ☐   22 ÷ 2 = ☐

50 ÷ 5 = ☐   70 ÷ 10 = ☐   5 ÷ 1 = ☐   25 ÷ 5 = ☐

55 ÷ 5 = ☐   110 ÷ 10 = ☐   18 ÷ 2 = ☐

Parent tip
If you timed Progress check 2, time this one to see if your child can complete the divisions more quickly.

Score: __ / 39

How much did you do?   Question 1

Circle the star
to show what
you have done.

Some

Most

All

Answers

Counting in 2s on a number line

Page 4
1 2, 4, 6, 8, 10
2 4, 6, 8, 10
3 14, 16, 18, 20, 22, 24
4 14, 16, 18, 20, 22, 24

Page 5
5 6, 8
    12, 20
    22, 24
6 Any two colours can be used.

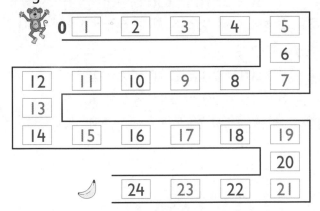

Counting in 5s on a number line

Page 6
1 5, 10, 15, 20
2 10, 15, 20, 25, 30, 35, 40, 45, 50
3 20, 25
    20, 30, 40
    25, 30, 50
    35, 55, 60

Page 7
4 The following squares should be coloured:
    10, 15, 20, 25, 30, 35, 40, 45, 50, 55, 60
5 5, 10, 15, 20, 25, 30
    35, 40, 45, 50, 55, 60
6 10, 15, 20, 25, 30, 35, 40, 45, 50, 55, 60

Counting in 10s on a number line

Page 8
1
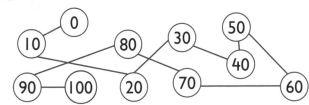

2 20, 30, 40, 50, 60, 70, 80, 90, 100
3 8 jumps of 10

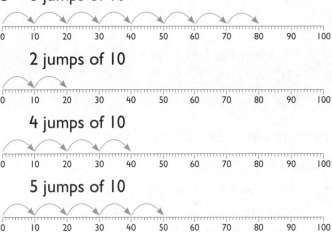

2 jumps of 10

4 jumps of 10

5 jumps of 10

Page 9
4 20, 30
    70, 80
5 40, 100
6 10, 40, 50
    40, 50, 70, 90
    80, 100, 110

Counting objects in 2s

Page 10
1 8
2 4, 12
3 2, 20

Page 11
4 18, 24
5 16
6 6p, 10p, 14p

Counting objects in 5s

Page 12
1 30
2 5, 50
3 35

Page 13
4 3 × 5 = 15, 8 × 5 = 40
5 60
6 10p, 20p, 30p

Counting objects in 10s

Page 14

1 40
2 20, 50
3 80

Page 15

4 $7 \times 10 = 70$, $1 \times 10 = 10$
5 120
6 30p, 50p, 90p

2s and 10s mixed practice

Page 16

1 Machine 1 (×2): 22, 4, 0, 16, 14
　Machine 2 (×10): 100, 20, 60, 0, 80
2 20 = red (body of bus), 10 = blue (windows),
　16 = grey (wheel trim, hubs and bumpers),
　30 = black (tyres), 0 = yellow (lights)
3 ✔, ✔, ✗
　✗, ✔, ✔

Progress check 1

Page 17

4 0, 80, 4, 0, 8, 90, 20, 14, 45, 120, 20, 40,
　24, 6, 60, 0, 30, 12, 10, 30, 35, 50, 16, 60,
　100, 5, 10, 10, 20, 15, 40, 22, 50, 70, 2, 25,
　55, 110, 18

2 times table arrays

Page 18

1 4, 4
2 8
3 16

Page 19

4 18
5 (4 more counters added to each row to
　give 2 rows of 11.) 22
6 (An array consisting of 2 rows of
　12 objects or 2 columns of 12 objects.)
　$12 \times 2 = 24$

5 times table arrays

Page 20

1 5
2 3, 15
3 5 columns of 7 squares coloured (35 in total)

Page 21

4 5×5
5

10 × 5　　8 × 5　　4 × 5　　3 × 5

10 times table arrays

Page 22

1 30
2 (2 more rows of 10 dots drawn to give
　4 rows of 10 in total.) 40
3 $8 \times 10 = 80$, $6 \times 10 = 60$, $3 \times 10 = 30$

Page 23

4 $2 \times 10 = 20$ and $10 \times 2 = 20$
　$5 \times 10 = 50$ and $10 \times 5 = 50$
5 ★ ★ ★ ★ ★ ★ ★ ★ ★ ★
　1×10

　4×10

　7×10
6 7 rows of 10 objects drawn to show 7×10.

Doubling numbers

Page 24

1 12, 16, 6
2 6, 4, 12, 2, 8, 10
3 Double 7 = 14, Double 9 = 18,
　Double 10 = 20

Page 25

4

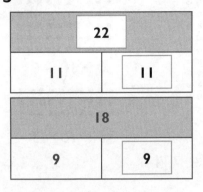

5 2 × 10 = 20, 2 × 12 = 24,
2 × 4 = 8, 2 × 9 = 18

6 Going in a clockwise direction: 8, 24, 16,
18, 22, 14, 20, 12, 2, 10

Sharing between 2

Page 26

1 5 fish

2 8

3 12

Page 27

4 10 and 10, 15 and 15

5 7 and 7, 16 and 16, 12 and 12, 20 and 20

6 18, 29, 30, 10, 22, 35

Sharing between 5

Page 28

1 3 written in each box

2 4 written in each box

Page 29

3 45 shared by 5 = 9, 10 shared by 5 = 2,
20 shared by 5 = 4

4 8 written in each box
5 written in each box
6 written in each box

5 7, 10, 9, 6, 8, 11

Sharing between 10

Page 30

1 2 written in each box

2 1 written in each box

Page 31

3 2 written in each box
5 written in each box
8 written in each box

4 1, 6, 3

5 10, 12, 7, 11

5s and 10s mixed practice

Page 32

1 15, 60, 40, 20, 35, 70, 45, 120, 55

2 Circles around the numbers: 5, 10, 15, 20,
25, 30, 35, 40, 45, 50, 55, 60, 65, 70, 75,
80, 85, 90, 95 and 100
Triangles around the numbers: 10, 20, 30,
40, 50, 60, 70, 80, 90 and 100

Progress check 2

Page 33

3 1, 8, 2, 2, 4, 9, 4, 7, 9, 12, 10, 8, 12, 3, 12,
5, 3, 6, 2, 6, 7, 5, 8, 6, 10, 1, 10, 1, 2, 3, 4,
11, 10, 7, 5, 5, 11, 11, 9

Halving numbers

Page 34

1 2, 3, 5

2 8, 12, 2

3 7 and 7, 10 and 10, 9 and 9

Page 35

4 11, 20, 45, 2 and 11, 2 and 20, 2 and 45

5 6, 5, 50, 7, 10, 9, 2, 20, 35, 30, 25, 11

6 12, 12, 10, 10, 20, 20, 7, 7, 15, 15, 40, 40

Counting backward on a number line

Page 36

1 5

2 12

3 5

Page 37

4 12, 8

5 7, 11

6 9, 4

Grouping in 2s

Page 38

1 3

2 4

3 6

Page 39

4 14 grouped into 2s = 7, 18 grouped into 2s
= 9, 20 grouped into 2s = 10, 22 grouped
into 2s = 11, 24 grouped into 2s = 12

5 8 = 4 groups of 2, 12 = 6 groups of 2,
4 = 2 groups of 2, 6 = 3 groups of 2

6 6, 2, 8, 1

Grouping in 5s

Page 40

1 3

2 5

3 7, 7

Page 41

4 2, 4

5

1	2	3	4	5	6	7	8	9	10
11	12	13	14	15	16	17	18	19	20
21	22	23	24	25	26	27	28	29	30
31	32	33	34	35	36	37	38	39	40
41	42	43	44	45	46	47	48	49	50
51	52	53	54	55	56	57	58	59	60

12

6 6, 11, 12, 8

Grouping in 10s

Page 42

1 2

2

1	2	3	4	5	6	7	8	9	10
11	12	13	14	15	16	17	18	19	20
21	22	23	24	25	26	27	28	29	30
31	32	33	34	35	36	37	38	39	40
41	42	43	44	45	46	47	48	49	50
51	52	53	54	55	56	57	58	59	60
61	62	63	64	65	66	67	68	69	70
71	72	73	74	75	76	77	78	79	80
81	82	83	84	85	86	87	88	89	90
91	92	93	94	95	96	97	98	99	100

10

3 4

Page 43

4 8, 8

5

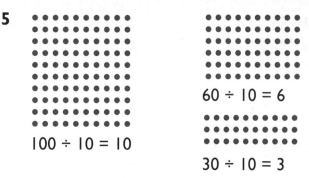

$100 \div 10 = 10$

$60 \div 10 = 6$

$30 \div 10 = 3$

6 9, 5, 9, 5, 7, 4, 7, 4

2s, 5s and 10s mixed practice

Page 44

1

11	20	56	12	87
70	3	30	61	40
6	25	37	10	15
35	99	5	49	80
1	14	18	24	29

A letter X shape

2 15, 2, 10, 25, 24, 18

3

× 2	× 5	× 10
12		
2	50	
50	70	
8	35	50
70	100	70
14	25	100
100	60	60
22	45	
60		

Progress check 3

Page 45

4 0, 80, 4, 0, 8, 90, 20, 14, 45, 120, 20, 40,
24, 6, 60, 0, 30, 12, 10, 30, 35, 50, 16, 60,
100, 5, 10, 10, 20, 15, 40, 22, 50, 70, 2, 25,
55, 110, 18

Problem solving and reasoning 1

Page 46

1 6p, 20p

2 7 cars

3 6 children

Page 47

4 12 packs
5 24 wheels
6 9 children

Problem solving and reasoning 2

Page 48

1 30p, 50p
2 15
3 10 teams

Page 49

4 £50
5 12 marbles
6 35 pens

Problem solving and reasoning 3

Page 50

1 20p, 80p
2 40 points
3 100 sweets

Page 51

4 8 classes
5 120 pins
6 60 crayons

Multiply and divide by 10

Page 52

1 20, 50, 70, 90
2 3, 4, 6, 8
3 60, 60, 6, 10, 10, 1, 120, 120, 12, 50, 50, 5

Page 53

4 ×10 and ÷10, ×10 and ÷10
   ÷10 and ×10, ÷10 and ×10
   ×10 and ÷10, ÷10 and ×10
5 12, 1, 50, 90, 6, 8, 30
6 80, 9, 50, 10, 10, 4, 30, 12, 60, 11, 20, 7, 120

Commutativity

Page 54

1 45, 5, 45, 20, 2, 20, 30, 10, 30
2 5, 10
3 7, 2, 9, 10

Page 55

4 40, 8, 40, 5, 90, 9, 90, 10
5 16, 2 × 8 = 16, 16 ÷ 8 = 2, 16 ÷ 2 = 8
   55, 5 × 11 = 55, 55 ÷ 5 = 11, 55 ÷ 11 = 5
6 7 × 10 = 70, 10 × 7 = 70, 70 ÷ 10 = 7,
   70 ÷ 7 = 10
   5 × 12 = 60, 12 × 5 = 60, 60 ÷ 5 = 12,
   60 ÷ 12 = 5

Exploring arrays and commutativity

Page 56

1

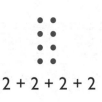

5 + 5 + 5   10 + 10

2 + 2 + 2 + 2

2

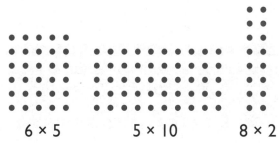

6 × 5   5 × 10   8 × 2

3 2, 9, 6

Page 57

4 2 groups of 5 and 5 groups of 2, 2 groups
   of 9 and 9 groups of 2, 5 groups of 7 and
   7 groups of 5
5 5 × 10 = 50, 50 ÷ 10 = 5
6 9 × 5 = 45, 5 × 9 = 45, 45 ÷ 5 = 9, 45 ÷ 9 = 5

Progress check 4

Page 58

1 1, 8, 2, 2, 4, 9, 4, 7, 9, 12, 10, 8, 12, 3, 12,
   5, 3, 6, 2, 6, 7, 5, 8, 6, 10, 1, 10, 1, 2, 3, 4,
   11, 10, 7, 5, 5, 11, 11, 9

Check your progress

- Shade in the stars on the progress certificate to show how much you did. Shade one star for every ⭐ you circled in this book.
- If you have shaded fewer than 20 stars go back to the pages where you circled Some ☆ or Most ⭐ and try those pages again.
- If you have shaded 20 or more stars, well done!

✂

Multiplication and division
Progress certificate

name _____ date _____

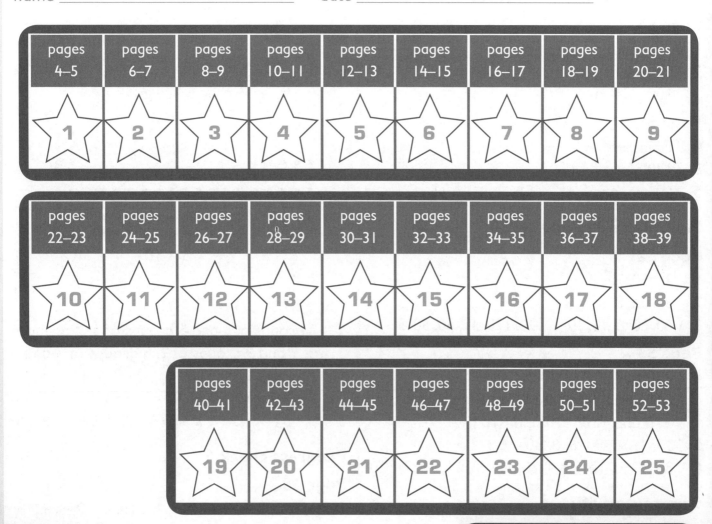

pages 4–5	pages 6–7	pages 8–9	pages 10–11	pages 12–13	pages 14–15	pages 16–17	pages 18–19	pages 20–21
1	2	3	4	5	6	7	8	9

pages 22–23	pages 24–25	pages 26–27	pages 28–29	pages 30–31	pages 32–33	pages 34–35	pages 36–37	pages 38–39
10	11	12	13	14	15	16	17	18

pages 40–41	pages 42–43	pages 44–45	pages 46–47	pages 48–49	pages 50–51	pages 52–53
19	20	21	22	23	24	25

pages 54–55	pages 56–57	page 58
26	27	28

Did you find all 26 mice?

(Including this one!)

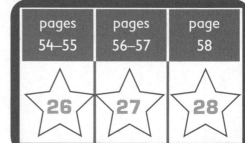